Quit Smoking...
Got Side Effects?

15 Remedies & 131 Tips to Overcome the Discomfort and Pain of Quitting Smoking

LELA BRYAN

© 2017 Lela Bryan

All rights reserved.

ISBN 978-1-500442-82-8

Table of Contents

Foreword ix

Acknowledgements. xi

Introduction. 1

Got Side Effects? 5
    Methods to Stop Smoking and the Severity of
    Side Effects of Each Method 6
    Severity of Side Effects Vary Per Method
    When Quitting Smoking 7
    Comparison Chart of Different Methods to
    Quit Smoking. 9
    Nicotine Replacement Therapy 11
    Common Side Effects of Quitting Smoking 12
    Quit Smoking Side Effects Timetable 14
    What Happens to Your Body When You
    Quit Smoking Timetable. 16

Digestion Side Effects. 19
    Nausea 19
    Diarrhea 20

 Gas or Flatulence 21
 Constipation. 21
 Homemade Laxative Recipe 23
 Alkaline/Acidic Foods. 24
 Highly Alkaline Foods. 25
 Highly Acidic Foods 26
 Acid Indigestion/Heartburn 27
 Stomach Pain 29

Irritability, Anger and Depression. 31
 Fluid Retention and Irritability 33
 Changes in Your Emotions 34
 Depression 37
 Excitement 38

Circulation Side Effects 41
 Tingly Fingers & Toes 41
 Itchiness 41
 Dizziness or Vertigo. 43
 Stiffness/Leg Pains. 43
 Sore Joints. 44
 Hot Flashes 44

Sleep Changes 47
 Dreams 47
 Vivid Dreams 47
 Night Sweats 48
 Stopping Smoking During Menopause 48
 Night Terrors 50

Lighter Sleep.. 50
Insomnia.. 50
Trouble Sleeping When on the Nicotine Patch?...... 51
Fatigue, Sleepiness and Drowsiness 51

Breathing 55
Gasping for Breath 55
Feeling Like Someone is Sitting on Your Chest 56
Chest Pains 57
Sinus Congestion 57
Natural Remedies for Sinus Problems 58
Coughing and Throat Clearing 58
Phlegm or Coughing Up Mucous 58
Hoarseness 59

Weight Changes.. 61
Sugar Cravings 61
Why Your Mouth Needs Attention When You Stop Smoking?.. 62
Water Retention/Bloating 63
Weight Gain 64

Skin Changes 67
Skin Blemishes 67
Hives... 68
Smelling Like Ammonia 68
Get Rid of Your Wrinkles 69

Other Side Effects—Headaches, Hot Flashes, Sore Mouth
and Gums 71
    Headache 71
    Hot Flashes 71
    Swollen Tonsils 72
    Sore Mouth and Gums 73
    Sore Tongue 74

Nicotine Replacement Therapy or NRT 77
    Understanding Nicotine Levels 78
    Stop Using Punch Words Such as "Cravings" ... 80
    Don't Substitute Anything for the Habit 81
    Nicotine Stresses Out the Heart 82

The Hidden Costs of Quitting Smoking 83
    Case Study #1: Robin J.—3 trips to the
    Emergency Room 84
    Case Study #2: Jenn L.—Several Doctor Visits 86
    Case Study #3: Lucy C.—No Doctor Visits 88

Over-the-Counter Remedies for the Side Effects
of Quitting Smoking 93
    Introducing for the First Time Ever 94
    Remedy for Gas or Flatulence 95
    Remedy for Heartburn or Acid Indigestion 96
    Remedy for Anxiety, Water Retention 96
    A Homeopathic Remedy for Insomnia 97
    Help for Fatigue 98

Remedy for Sore Mouth and Gums................ 99
Remedy for Getting Rid of Wrinkles 100

Resources 101
　The Bonus – This book made into videos 101
　Facebook Support Groups..................... 102
　7 Tips to Quit............................... 109
　About the Author 110
　Lela Bryan Contact Information 111

Foreword

In 2008 I entered a contest to write unique content for the internet. I wrote a Hubpage, which is like a blog or online magazine article. I didn't win the contest but my Hubpage has been very popular with over 500 comments and over 150,000 views.

The article covered the side effects of quitting smoking, how long a symptom could last, why it was happening and what were some inexpensive treatments that people could implement.

I realized from the comments, that I was the only one in the world explaining the side effects of quitting smoking and what could be done about them without taking drugs or going to the doctor or the emergency room.

I quit smoking in 1978. Since then, I have taught people all over the world how to quit smoking and stop chewing tobacco.

Lela Bryan
Alameda, CA
December, 2017

Acknowledgements

I want to thank all of the people who made comments on my original online research.

Thanks to J. Bruce Jones for your sage advice and support. Thanks to Don Crowther who set up the original contest on which this book is based. Thanks to Marianne Cenko for graphic design and editing.

Thanks to Jodi Bushnell who listens and supports me 100% of the time.

Introduction

I wrote this book so NO one would ever have to go through what Robin J. had to endure.

With just a little knowledge about how the process of quitting smoking affects the body, it could have saved Robin J., the doctors, the insurance company and the hospital thousands of dollars in needless tests, pain, time and anguish!

> *"I am so thankful I found your information. I quit a month ago and I went to the emergency room several times as I felt pressure in my chest, lower rib cage and tightness in my chest and throat. It would always ease up after I burped several times. I would also feel like I was having trouble breathing and the ER would tell me I was breathing fine and that I was having a panic/anxiety attack.*
>
> *They gave me blood tests, EKG'S, x-rays, a CAT scan of my throat, an ultra sound of my liver and gallbladder, a stool test, x-rays of my heart, lungs and abdomen, tons of steroid shots and antibiotics due to them saying I had bronchitis. They gave me*

5 rounds of antibiotics before they decided it must be viral.

I've had a sore mouth and throat that they said was Pharyngitis. They gave me Xanax for anxiety and told me to wait it out. My sinus's were all stuffed up and my ears hurt, but the doctor said my ears were not infected and to take some Zyrtec. They prescribed Prilosec for acid reflux.

All my joints and muscles are still sore. I have had trouble with my legs jumping while I try to sleep. I am lucky to sleep an hour before I wake up with dry throat and having to urinate. I have had to steadily drink water all night long.

I still have tingling in my hands and feet. At times I felt like I was losing my mind. I am just now getting to where I don't have as much gas and heartburn has disappeared.

With the gas gone, I no longer have pressure and tightness in my chest, under my ribs and in my throat. I still have it at times, but not all the time like it was for the first 3 weeks. I have even been told I may be going through menopause because I have hot flashes. I have had off and on dizziness, blurred vision and floaters. The doctor said I am fine.

The doctors treated me like I was going crazy because they couldn't find anything even after doing all the tests. I wish I would have quit gradually

INTRODUCTION

rather than cold turkey—I quit because I was getting shortness of breath and feeling badly. I want to be around to see my grandkids have kids!!! I smoked for 31 years and the urge to smoke has not been nearly as bad as I would have thought; but the side effects have been a nightmare."

—Robin J.

Editor's note—Look for a free bonus at the end of the book where you can join a support site.

1
Got Side Effects?

So you've quit smoking: You thought life would be better and your health would certainly improve, but not only do you not feel better, you feel worse than you did before, and now you're wondering how long these side effects and symptoms are going to last.

You can use this book as a reference book in order to know how long the side effects may last, what you can do to prevent or alleviate them and information, resources, and confidence to cope with the side effects of quitting smoking.

The information you find will save you time and the expense of doctor and emergency room visits, plus hundreds of dollars in unnecessary medical tests.

There are usually MORE physical and emotional side effects when stopping smoking with cold turkey methods. Not everyone experiences the same symptoms.

Jenn L. to Robin J.,
"I just read your post and I can't even begin to tell you how familiar your story sounds. I quit four months ago and I still have issues."

—Jenn L.

Methods to Stop Smoking and the Severity of Side Effects of Each Method

There are three main factors that affect the severity of side effects when you quit smoking.

1. The level of nicotine in your cigarettes or the nicotine level of the patch, gum, lozenges or e-cigarettes at the time that you quit smoking.
2. How long you take to detoxify or lower your nicotine level for the body and mind to adjust.
3. How long you work at changing your routines, behaviors and habits while you are still smoking. It takes 21-42 days to change a habit.

I'm going to compare the severity of the side effects of a smoker that smokes a pack of Marlboros, which is one of the most popular cigarettes in the US. The level of nicotine is 1.1 mg of nicotine.

Severity of Side Effects Vary Per Method When Quitting Smoking

Method	Nicotine Level When You Quit	Days to Lower Nicotine	Days to Change Behaviors	Severity of Side Effects
Nicotine Solutions	.1 mg nicotine	35 days	35 days	Low
Nicotine Patch	.7 mg nicotine (lowest level)	30 days	30 days	Medium
Nicotine Lozenges	.7 mg nicotine	30 days	30 days	Medium
Nicotine Gum	.7 mg nicotine	30 days	30 days	Medium
Nicotine Nasal Spray	.7 mg nicotine	30 days	30 days	Medium
Chantix (USA) Champix (outside USA)	22 mg nicotine	84 days	84 days	Medium to Severe
Allen Carr book	22 mg nicotine	21 days	21 days	Medium to Severe
Wellbutrin/ Zyban	22 mg nicotine	14 days	14 days	Severe

QUIT SMOKING... GOT SIDE EFFECTS?

Method	Nicotine Level When You Quit	Days to Lower Nicotine	Days to Change Behaviors	Severity of Side Effects
Hypnosis	22 mg nicotine	0 days	0 days	Severe
Acupuncture	22 mg nicotine	0 days	0 days	Severe
Cold Turkey	22 mg nicotine	0 days	0 days	Severe

Comparison Chart of Different Methods to Quit Smoking

	Interactive Group Support	Long Term Support	Deal With Stress	Change Thought Patterns	Disconnect Psychological Triggers	Change Behavior Patterns
Nicotine Solutions	X	X	X	X	X	X
Nicotine Patch						
Nicotine Lozenges						
Nicotine Gum						
Nicotine Nasal Spray						
Chantix (USA) Champix (outside USA)			X			
Allen Carr book			X	X	X	X
Wellbutrin/ Zyban			X			
Hypnosis			X	X	X	
Acupuncture						
Cold Turkey						

Comparison Chart of Different Methods to Quit Smoking

	Gradual Detox From Nicotine	Taught By A Former Smoker	Built-in Weight Controls	Multifaceted Approach	No Drugs	No Cold Turkey
Nicotine Solutions	X	X	X	X	X	X
Nicotine Patch	X					
Nicotine Lozenges	X					
Nicotine Gum	X					
Nicotine Nasal Spray	X					
Chantix (USA) Champix (outside USA)						
Allen Carr book					X	
Wellbutrin/ Zyban						
Hypnosis					X	
Acupuncture					X	
Cold Turkey					X	

Nicotine Replacement Therapy

In the nicotine replacement group below you are not smoking cigarettes but you still have significant levels of nicotine in your system. Even at the lowest dose of the products, the nicotine levels are still very high so it is still not giving the body and mind time to adjust and in essence are cold turkey.

- Nicotine patch
- Nicotine lozenges
- Nicotine nasal spray
- Nicotine gum

Common Side Effects of Quitting Smoking

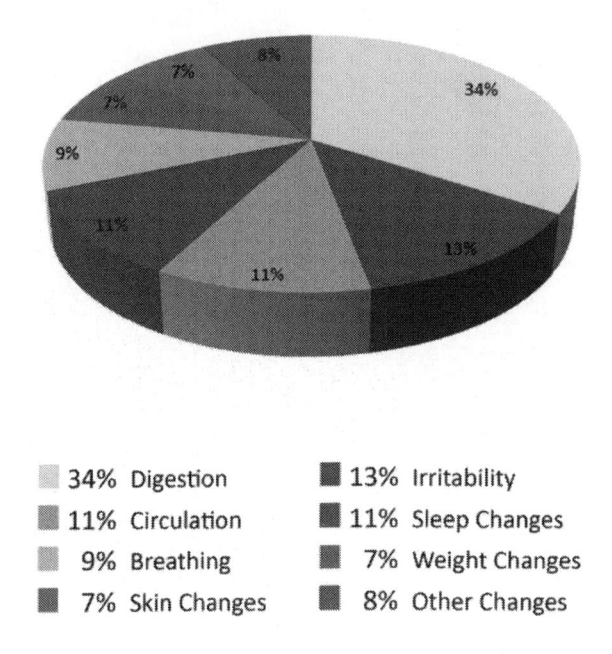

- 34% Digestion
- 11% Circulation
- 9% Breathing
- 7% Skin Changes
- 13% Irritability
- 11% Sleep Changes
- 7% Weight Changes
- 8% Other Changes

Thousands of smokers have been polled online since 2008 and here are the most frequently experienced side effects down to the least experienced side effects of quitting smoking.

Digestion 34%

"My biggest problems are digestive: heartburn, gas, nausea, diarrhea, constipation."

Irritability, Anger, Depression 13%

"The emotional shifts (depression, mood swings, irritability) are the most troubling."

Circulation 11%
"Circulation issues are the worst: dizziness, leg pain, itchiness, tingling and swelling."

Sleep Changes 11%
"I'm having the most trouble sleeping: fatigue, insomnia, and disturbing dreams."

Breathing 9%
"Breathing is the main issue: I'm having trouble with coughing, breathing, and phlegm."

Weight Changes 7%
"The weight gain bothers me the most."

Skin Changes 7%
"My skin (blemishes/hives) is bugging me."

Other Changes 8%
"My mouth hurts and I have a headache that won't go away."

QUIT SMOKING... GOT SIDE EFFECTS?

Quit Smoking Side Effects Timetable

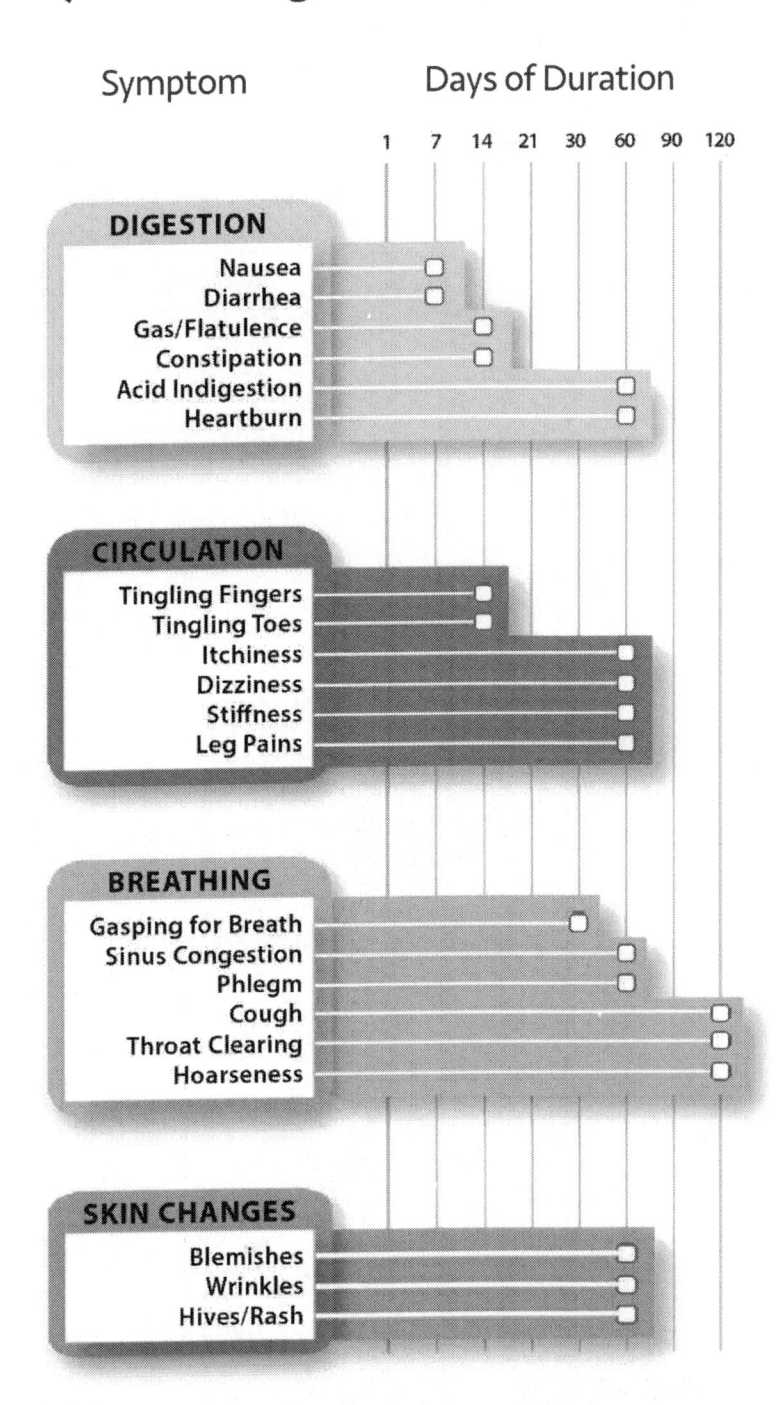

Symptom — Days of Duration

1 7 14 21 30 60 90 120

DIGESTION
- Nausea
- Diarrhea
- Gas/Flatulence
- Constipation
- Acid Indigestion
- Heartburn

CIRCULATION
- Tingling Fingers
- Tingling Toes
- Itchiness
- Dizziness
- Stiffness
- Leg Pains

BREATHING
- Gasping for Breath
- Sinus Congestion
- Phlegm
- Cough
- Throat Clearing
- Hoarseness

SKIN CHANGES
- Blemishes
- Wrinkles
- Hives/Rash

1: GOT SIDE EFFECTS?

Quit Smoking Side Effects Timetable,
continued

Symptom	Days of Duration

Days markers: 1, 7, 14, 21, 30, 60, 90, 120

IRRITABILITY
- Irritability — up to 90 days
- Anger — up to 90 days
- Depression — up to 90 days
- Euphoria — up to 90 days
- Lethargy — up to 90 days

SLEEP CHANGES
- Vivid Dreams — up to 21 days
- Nightmares — up to 21 days
- Lighter Sleep — up to 21 days
- Less Sleep Required — up to 21 days
- Sleepiness — up to 90 days
- Drowsiness — up to 90 days
- Fatigue — up to 90 days
- Insomnia — up to 90 days

WEIGHT CHANGES
- Sugar Cravings — up to 30 days
- Bloating — up to 30 days
- Water Retention — up to 60 days
- Slower Metabolism — up to 60 days

OTHER CHANGES
- Headache — up to 30 days
- Hot Flashes — up to 60 days
- Sore Tongue — up to 90 days
- Sore Mouth & Gums — up to 90 days

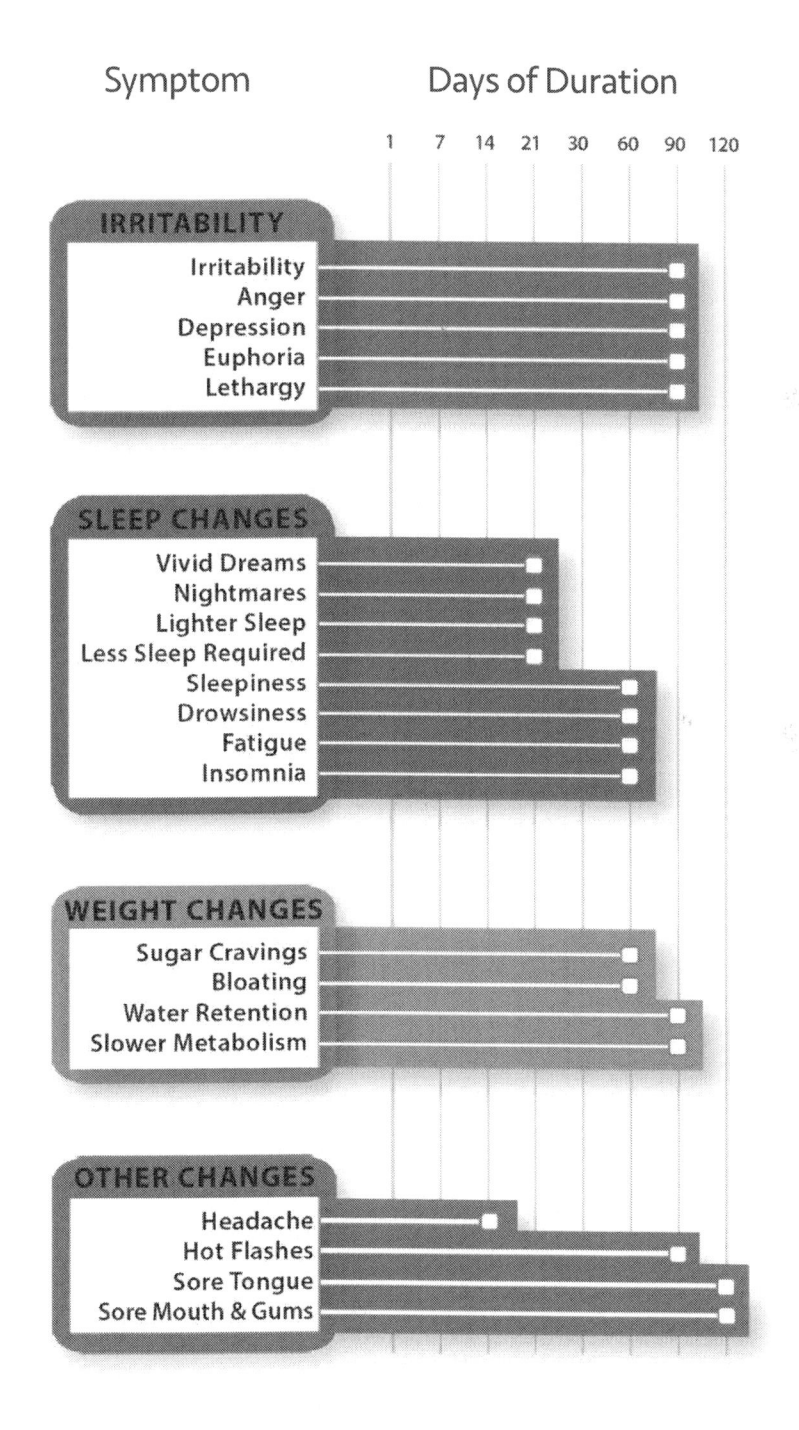

What Happens to Your Body When You Quit Smoking Timetable

After 20 Minutes
Blood pressure, pulse rate and the temperature of your hands and feet return.

After 8 Hours
Nicotine and carbon monoxide levels in blood reduce by half and oxygen levels return to normal.

12 Hours
Blood oxygen level has increased to normal.

24 Hours
Carbon monoxide levels have dropped to normal.

After 48 Hours
Carbon monoxide is eliminated from the body. Lungs start to clear out mucus and other smoking debris. Ability to taste and smell is greatly improved. Damaged nerve endings begin to regrow.

After 72 Hours
Breathing becomes easier. Bronchial tubes begin to relax and lung's functional abilities are starting to increase. Energy levels increase. Your entire body is free of nicotine.

10 Days–2 Weeks
Your circulation improves. Your addiction is no longer doing the talking. Blood circulation in your gums and teeth are now similar to that of a non-user.

After 3–9 Months
Coughs, wheezing and breathing problems improve as lung function increases by up to 10%.

After 5 Years
Risk of heart attack falls to about half compared with a person who is still smoking.

After 10 Years
Risk of lung cancer falls to half that of a smoker. Risk of cancer of the mouth, throat and declined.

15 Years
Your risk of coronary heart disease is now that of a person who has never smoked.

20 Years
Excess risk of death from all smoking related causes, including lung disease and cancer has now reduced to that of a person who has never smoked.

2
Digestion Side Effects
Symptoms • Duration • Treatment

Nausea

This symptom almost seems like the flu. The duration typically lasts about a week. The treatment would be to drink lots of water and a carbonated beverage—which should help.

> *"For the first 3 days I had headaches, nausea and diarrhea."*
>
> —Karen

> *"I've quit smoking (cold turkey) for more than 2 months. I smoked eighteen years. Now I am feeling dizziness, headache, vomiting, and body and muscle pain."*
>
> —Aman

Diarrhea

This symptom typically can last a few days. Try any over-the-counter remedy for diarrhea. The body is adjusting to the new digestive changes.

"I smoked for 17 years at a rate of 12-15 cigarettes per day. Four months back I stopped smoking cold turkey. Needless to say I have suffered enormously due to the lack of knowledge of the impact of cold turkey. My pains started 3 days after stopping. The inner lining of my mouth was sore. I had severe stomach problems (bloating, cramps lasting up to 8 weeks), diarrhea for a day, inability to hold onto food. The more I stressed about my symptoms, the worse my stomach problems got."

—Hishy

Digestion Symptoms

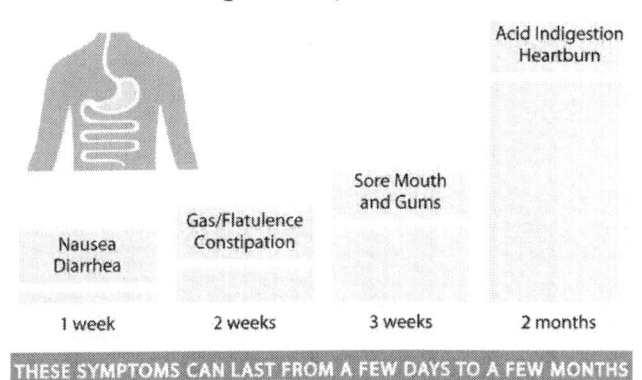

1 week	2 weeks	3 weeks	2 months
Nausea / Diarrhea	Gas/Flatulence / Constipation	Sore Mouth and Gums	Acid Indigestion / Heartburn

THESE SYMPTOMS CAN LAST FROM A FEW DAYS TO A FEW MONTHS

2: DIGESTION SIDE EFFECTS

Gas or Flatulence

Try to avoid eating gas-producing foods like beans, cabbage, or cauliflower. This symptom can last for several weeks.

Try Beano to relieve the symptoms of gas.

> *"I smoked 2 packs a day for 25 years and quit smoking cold turkey 3 weeks ago. Anyway, from my list of torments in the past 24 days: Enormous quantity of gas in my body (I have a slim/athletic build and I never had this problem before.) It's quite embarrassing because the smell is unbearable and it's not related to food."*
> —MickeyNBG

Constipation

This may last several weeks. Cigarettes act like a diuretic and also a laxative in the body so when you take nicotine away you can get constipated. You can use an over-the-counter remedy or make your own homemade laxative recipe that is natural and gentler on the body.

> *"Since I quit smoking cold turkey I have been dealing with bloating, fluid retention and strange pains in my intestines and gut. I have had heartburn all the time and a strange pain in my throat*

that comes and goes (sometimes, I can feel it up into my bottom teeth.)"

—Jenn L.

"I quit smoking about 9 weeks ago and at first, it was OK. After about 4 -5 weeks, I became so incredibly constipated that I believed I had rectal/bowel cancer. I have had a pelvic ultrasound and numerous x-rays because I am so **convinced** *I am dying. I have been trying to drink extra water and add fiber to my diet, but, I have also been suffering from heartburn and indigestion. I am still suffering from all three of these* **ailments.***"*

—jlove418

2: DIGESTION SIDE EFFECTS

Homemade Laxative Recipe

Ingredients	Instructions
8 oz. dried prunes 8 oz. raisins 8 oz. dried figs 2 oz. Senna tea leaves crushed or buy Senna tea bags and open up some bags (Senna leaves may be hard to find.) ¼ C lemon juice 2½ C water ¼ C brown sugar ½ C prune juice	Bring prunes, raisins, figs, Senna leaves, lemon juice and water to a boil. Boil for 15 to 20 minutes. Remove from heat and add brown sugar. Allow to cool. Using a mixer, turn into a smooth paste while gradually adding prune juice. Put in several plastic containers with lids and store in freezer. It will be the consistency of ice cream. Take 1 tablespoon every morning and evening day (Use it as a spread.)

Note—This recipe can be printed out from our website. www.nicotinesolutions.com/homemade-laxative-recipe/

Quit Smoking Side Effects Timetable

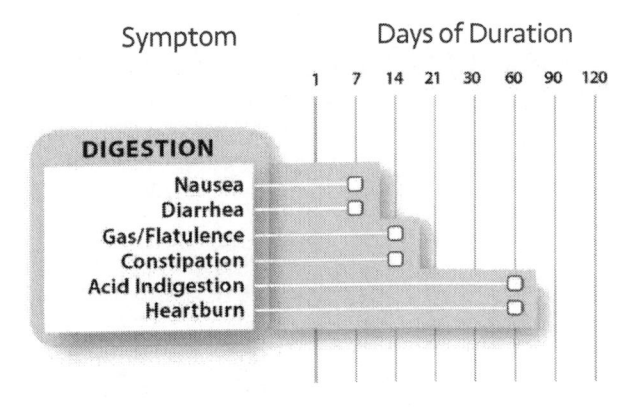

Symptom	Days of Duration

1 7 14 21 30 60 90 120

DIGESTION
- Nausea
- Diarrhea
- Gas/Flatulence
- Constipation
- Acid Indigestion
- Heartburn

Alkaline/Acidic Foods

If you are still on any form of nicotine replacement therapy (NRT) like the nicotine patch, gum, lozenge or e-cigarette, then you are not detoxifying from nicotine. When you smoked, your body used nicotine as a laxative or it was an "aid in digestion" so you are not out of the woods until you are completely off of the nicotine in any form.

What you are doing with the patch is giving your body nicotine with a different delivery system. I am not taking away anything from your accomplishment; I am just saying that you will still have to detoxify from nicotine when you stop using the patch.

Acid indigestion is aggravated by acidic foods. Try to avoid eating these. Eat highly alkaline-based foods to help with digestion. Here is a list of **highly alkaline foods that will help:**

Highly Alkaline Foods

Almond Milk	Green Beans
Artichokes	Kale
Arugula	Kelp
Asparagus	Leeks
Avocado	Lemon
Baby Potatoes	Lentils
Beans & Legumes	Lettuce
Broccoli	Lime
Brussels Sprouts	Mustard Greens
Butter beans	Okra
Cabbage	Onion
Carrot	Parsley
Cauliflower	Peas
Celery	Quinoa
Chives	Radish
Coconut	Red Onion
Collard	Soy Beans
Cucumber	Spinach
Endive	Sprouted Beans (all)
Garlic	Tomato
Ginger	Watercress
Goat's Milk	Zucchini
Grapefruit	

If you have heartburn or acid indigestion **avoid** eating the following highly acidic foods:

Highly Acidic Foods

Alcohol	Fish
Artificial Sweetener	Jam
Beef	Jelly
Black Tea	Mushrooms
Cheese	Pork
Chicken	Shellfish
Cocoa	Soy Sauce
Coffee	Sugar
Dairy	Syrup
Dried Fruit	Vinegar
Eggs	Yeast

2: DIGESTION SIDE EFFECTS

Acid Indigestion/Heartburn

If you had acid indigestion before you quit, it will probably get a bit worse and then it **should** go away. If you never had heartburn or acid indigestion this symptom can last for about 3 weeks to 3 months. Another name for acid reflux is called **Gastroesophageal** Reflux Disease or GERD which is a digestive disorder that affects the lower esophageal sphincter. Try Tums or DGL (Deglycyrrhizinated Licorice), which may help acid reflux too. This can be found in most health food stores or online.

"I stopped smoking 6 weeks ago by going cold turkey and now I am suffering with constipation and acid indigestion. I have been to my doctors so many times that I think he must have thought I was going crazy. My partner commented one weekend 'will I have to take you to the hospital this week?' and a friend said I may need counseling.

It really made me feel like I was going crazy, but I know I'm not crazy and just experiencing the effects of the nicotine (leaving my body) that I craved for 19 years."

—Emma

"I quit smoking cold turkey almost three weeks ago. My heartburn, sore throat and leg pains are worse. My pattern is to quit for a year and start

smoking again. I always feel so much better when I stop. I smell better and food tastes better, however, the heartburn kicks my butt. I think this time I have been scared straight with my health and will quit for good."

—Bella

"The heartburn has been constant for the last several weeks and really bothersome. I made an appointment with my family doctor and she sent me for an ultrasound, which came back normal and then we did an upper GI series that showed I had large acid reflux. My doctor then prescribed Prevacid and said I should take it for 3 months. My experience with heartburn throughout my life has been very minimal. But this heartburn after quitting has been a killer. I'm not sure what I should do. I'm not big on pills and worried that I will never be able to stop taking Prevacid if I start."

—Jenny

"My worst symptom was the acid indigestion and the itching!!!"

—Bridget

2: DIGESTION SIDE EFFECTS

Stomach Pain

This is due to a change in how the body processes food. It should only last a week or two.

Jenn L. to Robin J.,

"Since quitting smoking, I have had a pelvic ultrasound for lower abdominal pain and leg pain; I have had several chest x-rays for bone abnormalities and possible tumors. The only thing the x-rays showed were arthritis of the middle back, a curvature of the spine and issues with my neck. I have had two CBC's run and some other blood work done. (Editor's note: CBC stands for complete blood count). I have been to so many doctors since I quit to the point where I think most of them think I am crazy. I seem to be having all of the symptoms listed, but they are staggered."

—Jenn L.

"I stopped smoking 6 weeks ago by going cold turkey. This is the first time I have quit smoking and am so proud of myself, but I have suffered badly. I had palpitations, even went to the hospital on an EKG machine, all ok. Had all my blood tests done—all ok too. Felt so emotional at times, cried for no reason, tingles in my left arm, still have dizziness

but not as bad as when I first quit. I'm now suffering with constipation and acid indigestion."

—Emma

Over the years I have discovered many over-the-counter remedies for the side effects of quitting smoking.

Throughout the book I recommended different products that have been proven to relieve side effects and symptoms. I have combined 6 of them into a *Kick Butt Recovery Kit* that you can read about in the back of the book.

In this chapter on digestion I recommend Tums (an antacid) and Beano to help with flatulence or gas.

Included in the
Kick Butt Recovery Kit

Relief From:

- **Gas**
- **Heart burn**
- **Acid Indigestion**

3
Irritability, Anger and Depression
Symptoms • Duration • Treatment

TYPICALLY, SOME OF THE MOST INTENSE SIDE EFFECTS OF quitting smoking are emotional, such as anger, irritability, depression, euphoria and lethargy. These are mentioned many times as the main side effects people go through. There are a few things you can do physically and emotionally for these symptoms when you are in the process of quitting smoking or stopping chewing.

> *"No patch, no gum, no e-cigarette, nothing! Three weeks in; I feel like I am going to die. I have a combination of all withdrawal symptoms on the list. I have good days and bad. I can't wait to cough all this up—it's taking longer for that part. The irritability and anger only lasted a week. That was good*

because any longer and I'm sure someone would have taken me out."

—Olivia

"Well it's good to know I'm not the only one! I have quit for 4 months now. I'm ready to jack in my job, I'm so emotional. I'm rowing with anybody who doesn't share the same opinion."

—Lisa

"It's been about 5 months since I quit cold turkey. I have constant heartburn, my throat is sore, I can't sleep, and I'm cranky and plain ole bitchy. I've gained weight and feel very depressed; I am so depressed I can't even leave the house. I am now going from one doctor to another, doing sleep studies, depression clinics and various therapies. I really opened a can of worms with this, but I will give it another month. If I am not better, then I will start to smoke again. I just can't have my family living with through my turmoil too much longer, and I can't either."

—Debbie

Quit Smoking Side Effects Timetable

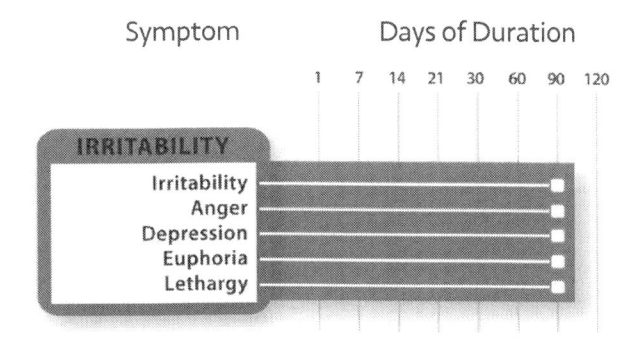

Symptom	Days of Duration

IRRITABILITY
- Irritability
- Anger
- Depression
- Euphoria
- Lethargy

(Duration scale: 1, 7, 14, 21, 30, 60, 90, 120 days)

Fluid Retention and Irritability

Fluid retention is one of the main causes of irritability. It can make you cranky and short tempered. You can reduce fluid retention by drinking as much water as possible (at least half you body weight in ounces) and cut down on foods that are high in sodium.

High sodium foods are soups, pickles, packaged and highly processed foods. Read the backs of packages to see the sodium content. Natural Diuretics (that keep your water balance in check) are parsley, horseradish, cantaloupe, watermelon, Brussels sprouts and lemon.

You can also use progesterone cream; it is a natural diuretic and helps with water retention.

A brand that I recommend in my Nicotine Solutions classes for men and women is Pro-Gest by Emerita. Just apply an amount, the size of a small pea, of cream to the fatty parts of your body in the morning and evening. Try to use a different location on your body every day.

You can buy Pro-Gest at most any health food store or it is one of the recommended products in the *Kick Butt Recovery Kit*.

> *"I hate the crying. I cried for days. Then I would cry some more because I was so angry at myself for crying. It felt like genuine grief and I would burst into tears and couldn't stop."*
>
> —Kelly

Changes in Your Emotions

After you have quit smoking, you need to teach people how they are going to treat you. In the past when you quit they probably said, "Oh you were nicer as a smoker" and then beg you to start smoking again because you were so cranky and nasty. Now you have to explain that you are going to handle life in a different way.

At first when you quit smoking, your emotions are on a roller coaster. You don't just feel sad; you are on the floor sobbing sad and if you are happy, you are jumping off the walls happy. If you are angry, you get angry at things that normally wouldn't bother you.

The reason your emotions are so exaggerated is that as a smoker, you have used smoking to express your emotions

3: IRRITABILITY, ANGER AND DEPRESSION

instead of actually feeling them. When I was a smoker, if I was mad at you I would smoke one cigarette and if I was really angry with you, I would smoke two cigarettes!

After you quit smoking, you have to actually feel your emotions. It can be very scary. Usually smokers have at least one main overriding emotion that they smoke for—such as anger, irritability, anxiety or even joy. When you quit smoking that one feeling will show up everywhere; you just have to dance with it and try it on and not be afraid of that emotion or feeling.

When I first quit smoking, I realized that the main reason that I used to smoke was for anger. I don't like showing anger; so smoking to avoid showing anger was perfect for me. After I quit smoking I changed my approach to dealing with anger. I told people more of what I was feeling, I confronted people more and I took up racquetball to get out my anger in a physical way. I still don't like to show anger, but I don't smoke for it.

Pro-Gest by Emerita can also be used as an antidepressant. It is in the kit at the back of the book.

Now that you have quit smoking you are starting to feel your emotions rather than cover them up with smoke. It feels strange at first to actually feel anger, sadness or joy rather than smoke for those feelings but it is actually much more effective to feel those emotions rather than to cover them up with smoke. Trust me there is life after smoking and it will take some time, but eventually it will all smooth out.

QUIT SMOKING... GOT SIDE EFFECTS?

I really like the book and the calendar called "Getting in Touch with your Inner Bitch." Sorry guys there are no male counterparts!

People ask "Is it more difficult for women to quit smoking than men?"

Women sometimes have a slightly more difficult time to stop smoking because when you quit smoking there is a hormonal change. Women naturally have more hormones than men and are usually more affected by quitting smoking.

Pro-Gest can help even out the hormonal change as well (Don't worry, I don't have stock in Emerita, but this is a great product for a number of side effects when you quit smoking.)

> *"11 days and the lethargy is the worst. I am a very motivated and energetic person and the lack of energy has been a problem. My ability to taste has changed. I love the fact that I no longer cough at night or in the morning. And YES...it has to be the smoker's idea to quit. Period. My guy has also decided to quit (a few days behind me but ok) so we are patient with each other. I am very proud of myself!"*
>
> —Michelle

Depression

Depression is a common side effect of stopping smoking, in the short and long term. It may feel like grief or the way you might feel if you lost a loved one. They say that quitters go through a period of mourning in the early stages of withdrawal. If it continues, take an herbal drug remedy called Sulfonil by Thorne.

> *"Yesterday was a month since I quit. I have tried so many strategies in the past to quit and they all failed, so this time I quit cold turkey. I have been struggling with anxiety and depression for the last 2 weeks. It has really started to wear me down. I don't have any desire to go back to smoking but I am not enjoying this either."*
>
> —Sam

Excitement

Many people experience excitement, anxiety and panic attacks. Your emotions are all over the board. Give yourself some time to smooth out.

> *"It is day 14 with quitting smoking cold turkey. Quitting smoking has been a nightmare for me. I turned 21 yesterday and I have been smoking for 9 years; I smoked about 30 a day. I'm having a hard time…I'm constantly tired all day with bad anxiety. I just force myself to do things and I am very very depressed. I have been thinking that maybe I have a terrible illness or cancer."*
>
> —Matt

Irritability Symptoms

Irritability
Anger
Depression
Euphoria
Lethargy

3 months

THESE SYMPTOMS CAN LAST FROM A FEW DAYS TO A FEW MONTHS

3: IRRITABILITY, ANGER AND DEPRESSION

"I was a smoker for 17 years and I quit cold turkey 15 days ago. Lately, I've been having an on-off fever, depression, high levels of anxiety...Is that normal?"

—Lloyd

"I am 46 years old and I smoked for 30 years. Wow it's been tough and I hope and pray it gets better. The am having panic attacks, can't sleep, heart palpitations and a lot of anxiety. I hope this goes away soon. I feel like I could climb a wall like Spiderman, wow I hope it gets better!!!!"

—Tammy

Included in the
Kick Butt Recovery Kit

Relief From:
- **Anxiety**
- **Irritability**

In this chapter on irritability, anger and depression we have included Pro-Gest in the *Kick Butt Recovery Kit* for relief from these symptoms.

4
Circulation Side Effects
Symptoms • Duration • Treatment

Tingly Fingers & Toes
Have patience. Having tingling fingers and toes is a good sign but it can be disconcerting if you don't know why it is happening. The good news is your circulation is improving and eventually everything will smooth out and you will feel better. This may last a few days to a couple of months.

Itchiness
Itchiness is possibly caused by increased circulation. It will last a few days to a couple of months.

> *"I quit smoking cold turkey a few months ago without doing any research or speaking to someone about it. Over the last few months I have felt like I was about to die and I am still feeling awful. I had*

a stress test and they took pictures of my heart, an MRI, several blood panels, urine samples, trips to the eye, ear, nose and throat doctor as well as to my GP who thought it could be my hormones. I kept explaining to the doctors that I was dizzy and my body hurt. One doctor said my mono came back, not the case. To doctor after doctor, I explained: "It feels like someone is ripping my skin out, I feel like I am going to pass out, extremely dizzy, congested, my fingers feel tingly, sometimes I feel like I can't feel them at all. I even have headaches and I have never had them before." One prescribed me Xanax and the other anti-depressant. Needless to say, my heart, blood work and everything came back ok. I cannot believe that stopping smoking can cause all of these symptoms. I felt like I was going to die, which did not make anything feel better."

—Rachel

Quit Smoking Side Effects Timetable

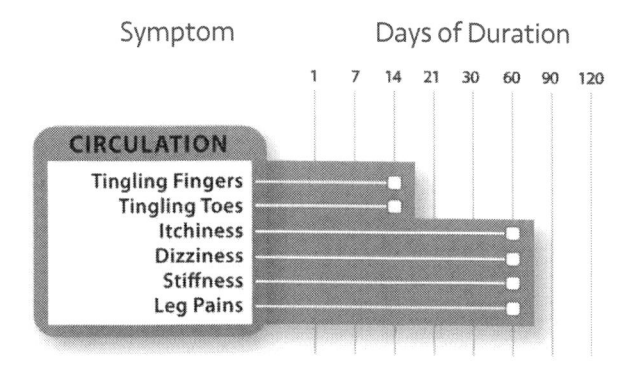

Symptom — Days of Duration

	1	7	14	21	30	60	90	120

CIRCULATION
- Tingling Fingers
- Tingling Toes
- Itchiness
- Dizziness
- Stiffness
- Leg Pains

Dizziness or Vertigo

Dizziness is probably due to increased circulation of oxygen to the brain. The symptoms should last a few days to a few months until your brain gets used to the extra oxygen. Give your body time to readjust to all the extra oxygen! You need to move a little more slowly and try to get up slowly rather than leap out of a chair.

Stiffness/Leg Pains

This means improved circulation. Remember you are changing at a cellular and muscular level. You will have temporary muscle changes. This almost feels like when you were having growing pains as a little kid. Take a hot bath, get a great massage, rub on Tiger Balm or just put your legs up to rest. This process may take several weeks, so give yourself a break!

Circulation Symptoms

Achiness
Dizziness
Stiffness
Leg Pains

Tingling Fingers and Toes

2 weeks   2 months

THESE SYMPTOMS CAN LAST FROM A FEW DAYS TO A FEW MONTHS

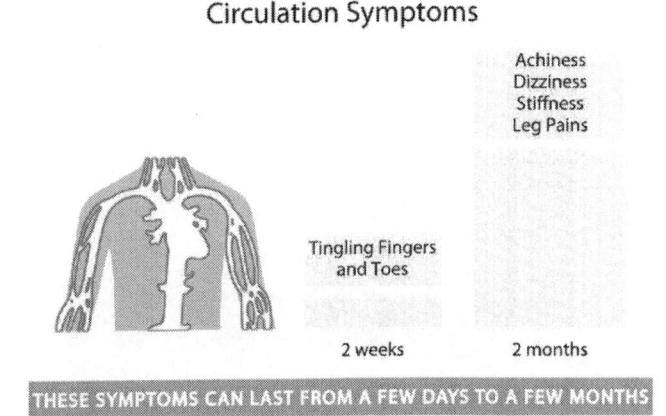

Sore Joints

Your body is building everywhere—even right down to all of your muscles. They are getting rid of the nicotine; there may be some soreness in your muscles and joints while your body rebuilds. This may take 2 or 3 weeks. Tiger Balm is good for stiff joints and muscles.

Hot Flashes

Some men and women experience hot flashes. This is due to the increased circulation and the hormonal change. Years ago when I lost weight, I got hot flashes. When I quit smoking I also got hot flashes and when I went through menopause I experienced the same hot flashes.

Men and women can try Pro-Gest which is natural progesterone cream by Emerita that can help with hot flashes. Hot Flashes can last a few days to a couple of months.

4: CIRCULATION SIDE EFFECTS

Included in the
Kick Butt Recovery Kit

Relief From:

- *Hot Flashes*

5
Sleep Changes
Symptoms • Duration • Treatment

Dreams
When you quit smoking, you may have vivid dreams, maybe even nightmares. Having dreams or even nightmares is a very good sign because it means that you are working out the problems of the day when sleeping and not smoking for them during the day. Everyone needs to dream and if you don't dream at night, you will need to daydream during the day.

Vivid Dreams
Although it is typical to have very vivid dreams or even nightmares when you quit smoking, I have heard that the dreams that you get from taking the drugs such as Zyban or Chantix are more "over the top" or a lot more dramatic than the dreams that you would get by using natural methods to stop smoking.

Night Sweats

You are sleeping lighter and having a different type of sleep. Many women going through menopause wonder if they are getting night sweats because of menopause or quitting smoking; night sweats could be a symptom of both.

Stopping Smoking During Menopause

There are many symptoms of menopause and quitting smoking that are exactly the same. Many times women that go through my Nicotine Solutions class to quit smoking ask is this a symptom from quitting smoking or from menopause. The answer usually is both.

Quit Smoking Side Effects Timetable

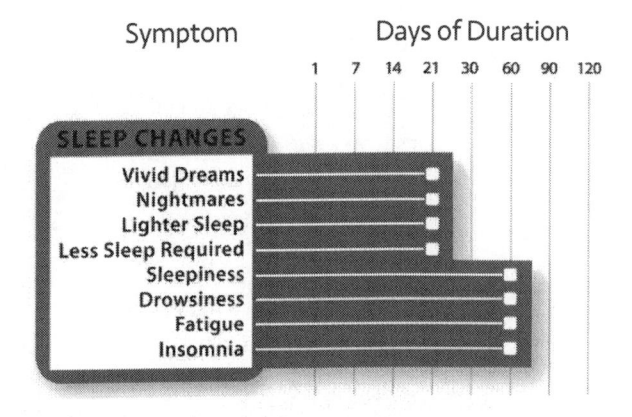

Symptom	Days of Duration
	1 7 14 21 30 60 90 120
SLEEP CHANGES	
Vivid Dreams	——
Nightmares	——
Lighter Sleep	——
Less Sleep Required	——
Sleepiness	————————
Drowsiness	————————
Fatigue	————————
Insomnia	————————

5: SLEEP CHANGES

"I smoked half a pack a day of Benson and Hedges and have quit cold turkey for 5 months now. I am only able to sleep for a few hours at a time with the lamplight on. This lasted 3 months. Heart turbulence lasted 1 1/2 weeks. Palpitations lasted 1 week. Shortness of breath lasted 3 weeks. Tingly fingers lasted a week in month 4. Pins and needles at odd times and is ongoing. I have had 4 EKG'S which were normal. 24 hr heart monitors—all normal, 13 doctor's appointments, heavy heartbeat sound for 6 days, no tar coughing as of yet in month 5 apart from the cigarette smell."

—Rymon

"I quit in the last two weeks and started a new job at the same time. I thought I was getting sick and developing a serious illness with night sweats, tiredness, sleepless nights, breathlessness, heavy legs and prickly feet. I am so relieved to know it's part of the detox process."

—Nadia M.

Night Terrors

Night terrors are very rare and may last a few days to a few weeks.

Lighter Sleep

After you quit smoking, you don't go into as deep a sleep as you did when you smoked. You tend to go into REM-Rapid Eye Movement (or a lighter dream state) more often. Usually REM occurs every ninety 90 minutes. Sometimes new non-smokers are not used to this "lighter" sleep and mistake the high quality REM state for not sleeping well when it is actually a better quality of sleep. It almost feels like you have been up all night. Your body will get used to the new higher quality, lighter sleep.

Insomnia

Getting used to the lighter quality of sleep can feel like you are not able to fall asleep or sleep as deeply as you used to sleep as a smoker.

Remember: fatigue is the number one trigger for smoking, so it is important to get your rest.

Hyland's makes Calms Forte and it is a great sleep aid. It is herbal and non-addictive. It makes you feel rested and not drugged in the morning. I have taken it and have told many students about it and even had my mom taking it!

Insomnia may last a couple of weeks up to 3 or 4 months. You can also use Pro-Gest for help with sleep.

5: SLEEP CHANGES

Trouble Sleeping When on the Nicotine Patch?

If you are still on the nicotine patch and having trouble sleeping, you might be on too high of a dosage of nicotine for you. Contrary to what the patch manufacturers tell you, you need to look up the nicotine level of the cigarettes that you were smoking to determine what level of nicotine patch you should use now. Please see the chapter on NRT for more information on this subject.

Pregnant women should not take ANY drugs to stop smoking.

Fatigue, Sleepiness and Drowsiness

Nicotine is a vasoconstrictor, constricting your blood vessels and stressing out your heart. As a smoker, your heart had to work harder, making your heart beat up to 10,000 more times a day.

Sleep Symptoms

Sleepiness
Drowsiness
Fatigue
Insomnia

Vivid Dreams
Nightmares
Lighter Sleep
Less Sleep

3 weeks   2 months

THESE SYMPTOMS CAN LAST FROM A FEW DAYS TO A FEW MONTHS

When you stop smoking, your heart rate slows down, thus slowing down your metabolism. When you are not getting that punch of nicotine, you may feel tired, sleepy, and lethargic. You might feel run down, almost as if you have a cold—in fact, some people refer to this feeling as the "smokers' flu" or "quitters' flu."

Don't worry, this is only temporary and will typically only last a few weeks. After that you should have more energy than when you smoked! But sometimes it takes longer to get your energy back. Your body remembers running on those shots of nicotine and getting those boosts of energy.

> *"I quit November 1, 2013. I am 21 years old and I have smoked since I was about 11. Where do I start? The first week was easy then two days after my fist daughter was born, week 2 of quitting smoking, I stated to get very fatigue. I mean I couldn't get out of bed —this lasted a week."*
>
> —Matt

When you quit, your body needs to adjust to its natural rhythm and sometimes it can feel like you are more tired than ever. Listen to your body, get rest and this too shall pass. Take catnaps, go to bed earlier, and drink fruit juice and water. If you have to drive or run heavy machinery, you can drink another cup of coffee or get some lozenges with caffeine in them to help keep you awake and safe. Enerjets are coffee flavored lozenge

5: SLEEP CHANGES

with caffeine in them and should keep you awake.

Remember fatigue is one of the chief causes of smoking, so it is important to get your rest. Enerjets Wake Up Energy Booster Drops are made by Chilton Labs and are included in the *Kick Butt Recovery Kit*.

Included in the
Kick Butt Recovery Kit

Relief From:
- **Anxiety**
- **Irritability**

6
Breathing
Symptoms • Duration • Treatment

Gasping for Breath

Breathlessness or having the feeling that you can't catch your breath—when you first quit smoking you are starting to breathe very deeply for the first time since you started smoking. As a smoker you were breathing deeply with smoke and now you are doing deep breathing with oxygen. When you first quit it might seem like you just can't get enough oxygen or you are actually feeling like you are almost going to hyperventilate. This typically only lasts for about a couple of weeks while you are learning to breathe deeply on your own without smoke.

Quit Smoking Side Effects Timetable

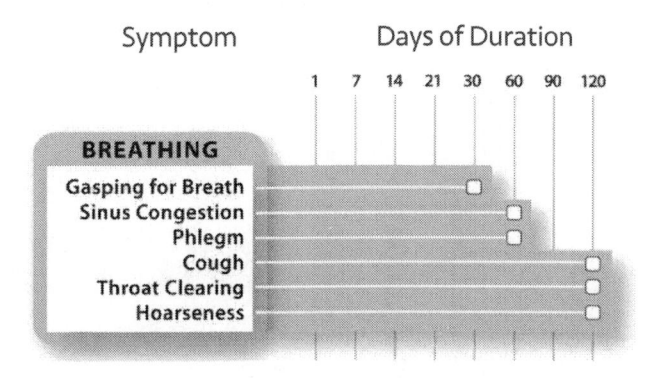

Symptom	Days of Duration

BREATHING
- Gasping for Breath
- Sinus Congestion
- Phlegm
- Cough
- Throat Clearing
- Hoarseness

Feeling Like Someone is Sitting on Your Chest

This can last only about a week or two. It is very disconcerting but it is nothing to worry about because it is temporary.

> "I bought my last pack 2 weeks ago and had my last cigarette 3 days ago. I am having horrible anxiety attacks and pain in my knees and legs. Right now it is easier to breathe through the mouth than the nose. I am occasionally lightheaded. I smoked for about 20 years. The hardest symptoms to deal with are the difficulty breathing through the nose and the anxiety."
>
> —Gretchen

Chest Pains

As the body rebuilds some people get a feeling of tightness in their chest or even heart palpitations. This is common and it should go away in a couple of weeks.

While you smoked you actually were doing deep breathing (with smoke.) Now that you have stopped smoking, you need to give it a little time to adjust and do deep breathing with oxygen. You can even practice doing breathing exercises.

Sinus Congestion

Sinus congestion is usually caused by a clearing out of the sinuses. It is almost as if (for a short period of time) someone has turned on a little water hose in your head.

Take an over-the-counter medication until the "dripping" stops or use a Neti Pot to help clear things out. This symptom may last up to 2 months.

Breathing Symptoms

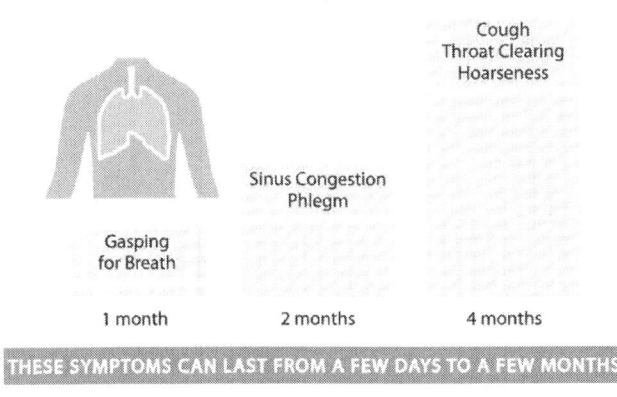

1 month	2 months	4 months
Gasping for Breath	Sinus Congestion Phlegm	Cough Throat Clearing Hoarseness

THESE SYMPTOMS CAN LAST FROM A FEW DAYS TO A FEW MONTHS

Natural Remedies for Sinus Problems

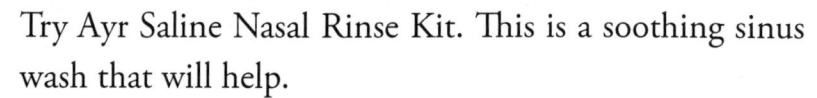

Try Ayr Saline Nasal Rinse Kit. This is a soothing sinus wash that will help.

Coughing and Throat Clearing

Coughing or throat clearing is due to reactivated cilia in your lungs. Cilia are the little hair like sweepers in the lungs that remove debris. When you cough you reactivate the cilia and they begin to work again. The coughing and throat clearing can last for a few days up to three or four months.

Phlegm or Coughing Up Mucous

Tar is a residue of tobacco. When you smoke nicotine tar is the residue that immobilizes the lung cilia. The tar tramples down the cilia almost as if you had poured molasses on a wheat field. The tar resin even looks like molasses! When you are coughing it is the body's way of clearing out the lungs—you are trying to cough out the tar.

The amount of tar you need to clear is determined by the amount of nicotine in your brand of cigarette. You can see the way this works by the following example which shows the amount of tar vs. nicotine contained in one cigarette:

Marlboro	100 filter hard pack	16 mg tar	1.1 mg nicotine
Carlton	100 filter hard pack	1 mg tar	.1 mg nicotine

Phlegm and coughing up mucous is a good sign that your lungs are clearing out the tar. It can last a couple of months. Since we can't get a vacuum down into the lungs—coughing up the debris is a good thing. Please see page 54 for more nicotine content.

> *"I woke up this morning feeling like I was short of breath and wheezing. I have not smoked in 5 weeks and 4 days now, but out of the clear blue could not breath well and I have used my inhaler all day every 4 hours due to having breathing difficulties I am starting to wonder if it's too late for me to quit and that I will only get worse? I cough up bits of yellow with light brown dots in it or just light yellow mucus. It is really thick. There are times it is like small pieces of mucus kind of shaped like a pencil eraser."*
> —Robin J

Hoarseness

Hoarseness often occurs because the soft tissues of your throat are being regenerated and the new non-smoker is getting some tender "baby" tissue—it is almost like when a baby is teething. This may last several months. Use lozenges or whatever you would do for a sore throat. Hot tea with lemon and honey can help.

You can also try Vademecum. You put a few drops in some hot water and gargle. I have used this for years and it really helps a sore throat. This symptom may last a few weeks up to 3 months.

7
Weight Changes
Symptoms • Duration • Treatment

Sugar Cravings

Most smokers smoke right after a meal. It has to do with your blood sugar. Some smokers that have quit want to duplicate the experience of the sugar lift after a meal so they might get sugar cravings.

> *"I smoked 40 hard years. Owing to a nasty upper respiratory infection, God granted me 2 days of no need to smoke (probably the only way I could quit.) I've experienced a large weight gain (30+ pounds), shortness of breath, and swelling."*
>
> —Dave

The new non-smoker will usually gain weight when they quit smoking because they typically substitute candy, gum, taffy, lemon drops, or pie for the habit.

Don't substitute anything for the habit; even it doesn't have calories like putting a toothpick in your mouth or chewing on pencils. You don't want to feed the habit in any way; let the habit die of neglect.

Why Your Mouth Needs Attention When You Stop Smoking?

The reason most people tend to substitute food or a toothpick for smoking is because your mouth wants attention! Your mouth becomes like its own zip code. Your mouth starts saying, "give me candy, give me food, give me gum, pie anything!" If you smoked 30 cigarettes a day, this is how many attentions to your mouth you would make:

```
    30 /day    x  10 days    =        300 attentions
   300 /day    x 365 days    =    109,500 attentions
109,500 /year  x  20 years   =  2,000,000 attentions
```

STOP giving your mouth attention by substituting food for the habit.

There is nothing sadder to me that seeing someone who has quit smoking 10 years ago and they still have a toothpick hanging out of their mouth or they are sucking on lemon drops! It is like someone has quit drinking but they still exhibit all of the old behaviors of drinking—called a "dry drunk".

In the Nicotine Solutions program, my students give their mouth attention in a different way. Instead of smoking, they brush their teeth and floss to get food particles out of their mouth so they won't be triggered to smoke.

When you quit smoking, try to stick to 3 meals a day that have more protein and fewer foods with sugar or fat for the first couple of months.

Water Retention/Bloating

Most smokers that quit smoking experience a 3 to 7 pound water weight gain. You might notice that your pants are getting tight. You can make sure that the water retention doesn't turn into fat by drinking a lot more water and staying away from processed foods and foods that are high in salt.

Avoid foods salty food, like potato chips and pretzels, for a couple of months. Another thing to do to avoid gaining weight is to start to exercise more.

Quit Smoking Side Effects Timetable

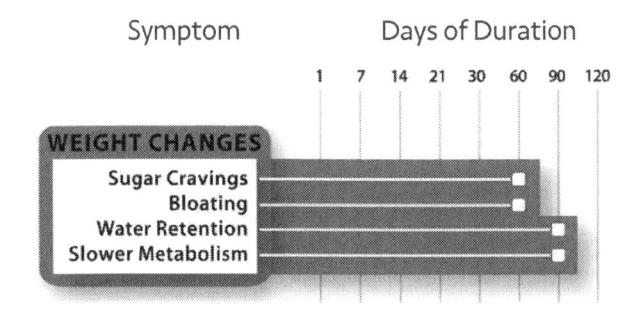

Symptom	Days of Duration
	1 7 14 21 30 60 90 120
WEIGHT CHANGES	
Sugar Cravings	———————————□ (60)
Bloating	———————————□ (60)
Water Retention	——————————————□ (90)
Slower Metabolism	——————————————□ (90)

> *"I really need to know if all my symptoms are from stopping smoking—I stopped smoking around 6 months ago and for the first 5 months I felt great and had no problems. Now I'm getting shortness of breath, stiff muscles and a lot of bloating around my waist…Is this all because of stopping smoking? It is reassuring to know it is from quitting cold turkey and that I'm not dying at 25!!"*
>
> —Emma

Weight Gain

There is a metabolism change when you stop smoking.

As a "smoker" or a "chewer" your heart rate beats 10,000 more beats a day when you smoke. Nicotine stresses out your heart and makes your heart beat harder—just to pump the blood through.

Weight Changes

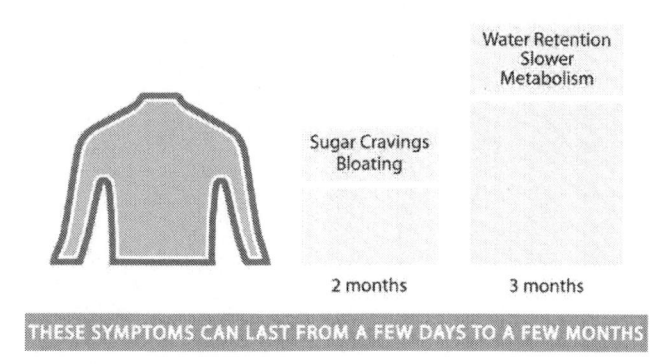

	Sugar Cravings Bloating	Water Retention Slower Metabolism
	2 months	3 months

THESE SYMPTOMS CAN LAST FROM A FEW DAYS TO A FEW MONTHS

7: WEIGHT CHANGES

10,000 beats a day of your heart is not a lot of calories, but over time it can add up to a three to seven pound temporary water weight gain.

Changes in your metabolism don't happen all at once and that is why cold turkey doesn't work very well to stop smoking. Cold turkey is abrupt and it is very hard for the body to adjust. If you don't want your temporary water weight gain to turn to permanent fat gain, start exercising more, eat less processed foods, drink lots of water and don't substitute anything for the cigarette.

Pro-Gest by Emerita can help the body use fat for energy and also works to normalize blood sugar levels. I have included Pro-Gest in the *Kick Butt Recovery Kit*.

Included in the
Kick Butt Recovery Kit

Help With:
- **Weight Gain**

8
Skin Changes
Symptoms • Duration • Treatment

Skin Blemishes

You would think that everything would start to improve when you quit smoking. But no! It will improve eventually, but not right away.

Your body is getting rid of toxins, and you may get acne, blemishes, or a rash after you quit. These may last about a month or two and then your skin should begin to look better than it did before.

There is no real treatment for skin breakouts but just know it is probably temporary and should go away in a couple of months.

"I quit smoking 8 days ago. I started when I was 11. It's been 24 years. I am doing it cold turkey. Pretty sure I am going to die from itching. Good to

know its common, thought I picked up an allergy to my wife for a minute there."

—Sam S.

Hives

Hives can be due to nerves from quitting cold turkey or the quick detoxification of nicotine from the body. It should go away within a couple of weeks but may last up to two months.

Smelling Like Ammonia

I have only heard of a couple of cases of people that have quit smelling like ammonia. The main thing to do for this is to stop eating acidic foods such as red meat, coffee and alcohol. Drinking lots of water will help.

Smoking Side Effects Timetable

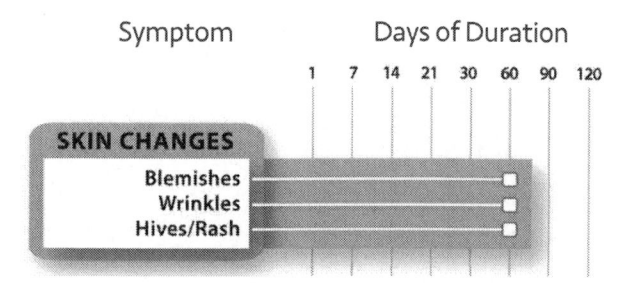

Symptom	Days of Duration
	1 7 14 21 30 60 90 120
SKIN CHANGES	
Blemishes	
Wrinkles	
Hives/Rash	

8: SKIN CHANGES

"I am on day 5 and I have horrible hives! It started with an itchy scalp, then neck, suddenly I had itchy hives up and down my body. I haven't been using any nicotine replacement but I was put on Wellbutrin about 3 weeks ago to help quit and boost my mood. I went to the ER because it was so intense and they want me to stop the medication."

—Lauren R.

Get Rid of Your Wrinkles

Now that you have quit smoking, I'm sure you probably want to get rid of your wrinkles. If you have been a smoker and are trying to get rid of wrinkles it can be different than getting rid of age related wrinkles.

I am looking for wrinkle product testers that have either quit smoking or are still smoking that want to get rid of their wrinkles. You will be required to take before and after pictures and you will need to buy the products. I can get some products as samples if you are a tester.

There will be some sample products, discounts, free coaching and webinars from Estheticians and contests and drawings to win your favorite products.

If you are interested in being a beta tester to try products that will get rid of smoking related wrinkles, email us at easeout@nicotinesolutions.com.

"I quit smoking 2 months ago on my birthday. It was a present to myself. I quit cold turkey no drugs or anything else and surprisingly I had no adverse emotional reactions, no anxiety or cravings or change in attitude. Unfortunately, I have been having skin problems. The acne isn't completely horrible but I've been getting red patches on my face and rashes. The skin on my scalp is peeling off horribly and itches like crazy, even after having a shower. I changed my products 2 weeks ago but it still hasn't helped. My eczema, which is usually very mild and shows up rarely with a small patch or two on my legs or feet has gone crazy with multiple patches on my lower body (more than 10.) I've used my eczema cream to help clear everything up; the rashes and red skin are easily manageable; it's the itchy peeling scalp that's bothering me the most! I hope it goes away soon."

—Mich

Skin Symptoms

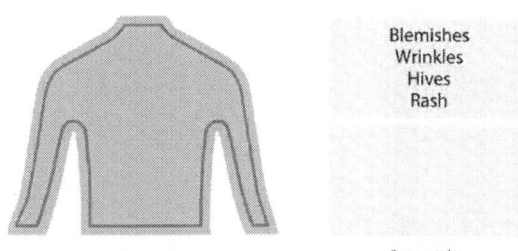

Blemishes
Wrinkles
Hives
Rash

2 months

THESE SYMPTOMS CAN LAST FROM A FEW DAYS TO A FEW MONTHS

9
Other Side Effects— Headaches, Hot Flashes, Sore Mouth and Gums
Symptoms • Duration • Treatment

Headache

Cutting down on caffeine usually causes headaches. Don't try to quit smoking and cut out caffeine at the same time. Increase your caffeine and it should go away in a week. Sometimes headaches will be caused by quitting smoking and in this case just take aspirin for a week or two and the headache should go away.

Hot Flashes

I had hot flashes when I quit smoking in 1978. I would have smoked in the shower if I could have kept them lit. There is a hormone change when you quit smoking for both men and women.

QUIT SMOKING... GOT SIDE EFFECTS?

When you quit smoking, hot flashes should only last a few weeks and you can use a natural progesterone cream. Rub a 1/4 tsp. of the cream on a fatty part of your body in the morning and in the evening.

I recommend a natural progesterone cream called *Pro-Gest made by Emerita because both men and women can use it. It doesn't have other ingredients in it like Black Cohosh and it is natural. (It is NOT hormone replacement therapy or HRT). Pro-Gest is found in the *Kick Butt Recovery Kit*.

Note for men: You will not grow breasts if you rub on this cream! If you have been a smoker, natural progesterone cream will also help with osteoporosis. Smoking is one of the main causes of osteoporosis.

Swollen Tonsils

Some people experience swollen tonsils and this can last up to a month.

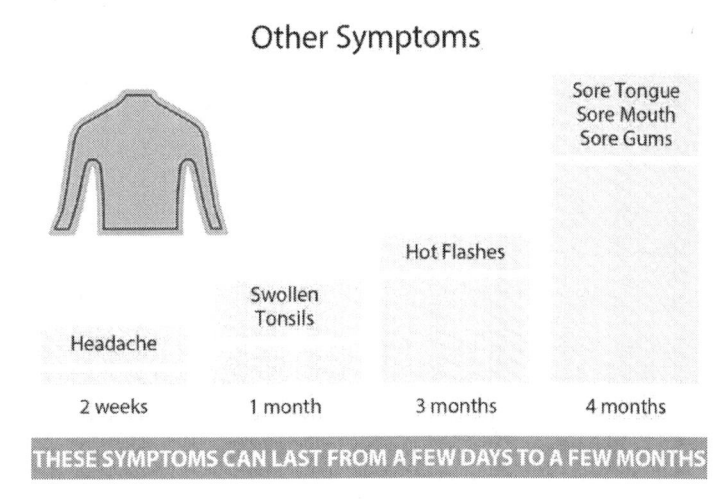

Other Symptoms

Headache	Swollen Tonsils	Hot Flashes	Sore Tongue / Sore Mouth / Sore Gums
2 weeks	1 month	3 months	4 months

THESE SYMPTOMS CAN LAST FROM A FEW DAYS TO A FEW MONTHS

Sore Mouth and Gums

When you smoked, you were literally smoking your gums and throat. Your gums and tissues built up a crust just like if you were smoking a salmon. When you quit smoking that old, hard crusty tissue sloughs off and in its place you will get new, baby tissue, almost like when a baby is teething.

Only about 1 out of 30 people that quit smoking or chewing get sore mouth or gums but if you are affected by this symptom your mouth will feel like it is hot and on fire.

Please don't suffer with this symptom as it may last as long as three or four months. A student in one of my classes had to have her dentures relined because there was a change in the shape of her gums from quitting smoking.

> *"I quit smoking cold turkey. It has been 60 days since my last smoke. I used to smoke two packs a day and have been a smoker for the last 32 years....the only side effect I had was bleeding gums for about 6 weeks."*
>
> —Kamal K.

Smoking Side Effects Timetable

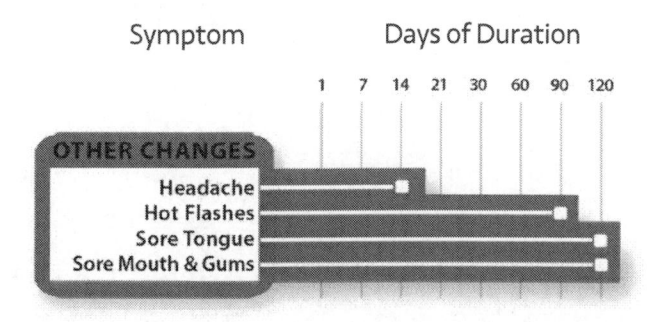

Symptom	Days of Duration
	1 7 14 21 30 60 90 120

OTHER CHANGES
- Headache
- Hot Flashes
- Sore Tongue
- Sore Mouth & Gums

Try Life Brand Oral Wound Cleanser (formerly known as Amosan) for sore mouth, gums and tongue. It is a soothing mouth-rinse. It comes as a powder and you mix it with water and rinse. It is very soothing and relieves a sore mouth. *Life Brand Oral Wound Cleanser is found in the *Kick Butt Recovery Kit*.

Sore Tongue

I recommend Life Brand Oral Wound Cleanser and it should soothe your tongue and this will last only a week or two.

> "Its day 4—I'm 22 years old and have been smoking for 6 years. The symptoms I'm getting are anxiety, sore tongue and throat like a burning feeling and cannot sleep."
>
> —Lenny

9: OTHER SIDE EFFECTS—HEADACHES, HOT FLASHES, SORE MOUTH AND GUMS

Included in the
Kick Butt Recovery Kit

Relief From:
- *Hot Flashes*
- *Sore Mouth & Gums*

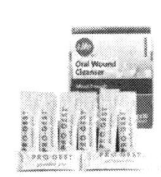

10
Nicotine Replacement Therapy or NRT

IF YOU HAVE QUIT WITH THE NICOTINE PATCH, GUM, LOZENGES, nasal spray or the e-cigarette then you have used nicotine replacement therapy to quit smoking.

You will probably experience some more side effects because you still have nicotine in your system.

Here is a question from Suzq88 who has quit smoking but is still on the patch:

> *"I am on day 17 after smoking a pack a day for 30 years. I have been using the patch. I chose to start at step 2 (14 mg). I noticed pretty bad cravings on days 12-15 but I try to remember why I quit.*
>
> *My biggest problem was around day 10. I became very congested with a severe headache, the worst I've ever had, along with facial pain and neck stiffness. I truly thought I had a sinus infection as I*

suffer with year round allergies already. It settled a little on day 13-14 but ramped back up and now I have all of it again plus ear pain and pain in my eyes along with dizziness; it is kind of like a zap in my brain from time to time.

I have been taking my allergy medications, sprays and nasal washes plus 3 ibuprofen and 2 Tylenol 2-3 times a day. It barely makes a dent.

"I am in this for the long haul, and will NOT fail, but a little relief from the headache at least would help for sure!!"

—Suzq88

If you have quit smoking but are on some form of nicotine replacement therapy then you are still dealing with the nicotine addiction and withdrawal.

When you drop from one nicotine level to a lower level it will still create a reaction. For some people, it feels like they are coming down with the flu. You don't have the flu, but it really feels like it.

Understanding Nicotine Levels

Suzq88 had a variety of symptoms and the crushing headache was the worst. This can have two possible causes. The first cause is from an abrupt drop in the amount of nicotine you are putting in the body. There are about 3 levels of nicotine replacement in the patches, gum lozenges and e-cigarettes.

10: NICOTINE REPLACEMENT THERAPY OR NRT

Nicotine Levels Per Day

Highest level	21 mg	nicotine per day
Medium level	14 mg	nicotine per day
Lowest level	7 mg	nicotine per day

What really matters is the nicotine content of the cigarette, not how many you smoke. Depending on your brand, the nicotine level will vary.

1 Pack a Day (20 cigarettes)

Carlton	.10 mg x 20	2 mg nicotine
American Spirits	1.92 mg x 20	38 mg nicotine
Marlboro 100	1.20 mg x 20	24 mg nicotine
Winston 100	1.20 mg x 20	24 mg nicotine

1/2 Pack a Day (10 cigarettes)

Carlton	.1 mg x 10	1 mg nicotine
American Spirits	1.92 mg x 10	19 mg nicotine
Marlboro 100	1.2 mg x 10	12 mg nicotine
Winston 100	1.2 mg x 10	12 mg nicotine

If Suzq88 used to smoke a pack a day of Marlboro's or Winston's (which are the two most popular cigarettes in the US) then she would be going from 24 mg of nicotine a day to 14 mg of nicotine because she chose to start at step 2 (14 mg) nicotine.

Depending on the strength of the nicotine in the cigarettes, you will probably have more symptoms and detoxification to work through. Nicotine is out of the system in 72 hours but the body takes a lot of time to recover from the shock of cold turkey.

The second possible cause of a headache is cutting down on caffeine. I don't recommend cutting down on caffeine while you are quitting smoking.

If you are still on the patch and stepping down on your nicotine level, then try to keep the same caffeine level throughout the process. There is plenty of time to lower your caffeine levels after you quit smoking. Don't try to do everything all at once. Work on cutting down your caffeine levels at least six months to a year after you have quit smoking. It is torture to do them together.

Stop Using Punch Words Such as "Cravings"

One of the lessons that I teach to students (in my Nicotine Solutions classes) who learn to quit smoking or chewing is that words are powerful. When you say words like 'I had a craving for a cigarette' or 'I had an urge' or 'I need a cigarette', it sounds ok on the outside of your brain. On the inside of your brain you hear those words differently. The punch words sound like Darth Vader is saying them and those words can grab you and control you like a rag doll.

In order to not be controlled by punch words you can stop using words like urge, craving, need, desire, want and substitute the word thought. So you had a thought. Big deal so you had a thought. Thoughts don't grab you and shake you or control you or throw you on the ceiling and then drop you on the floor. Thoughts just last a few moments and are just thoughts. You can deal with thoughts.

Having reasons to quit that are related to your ego are important in your quitting process.

You will be more successful when you quit if you have reasons that are specific and measureable and important to your ego; such as my breath will smell better, I won't smell like smoke, I can run up the flight of stairs without wheezing or my kids or grandkids will finally get off my back.

If you are quitting for someone else, it will usually backfire because the minute they do something wrong or disappoint you in some way, then you will go back to smoking to spite them and you will say something like 'look what I did for you.'

Don't Substitute Anything for the Habit

Do NOT substitute anything for the habit like candy, gum, toothpicks, lemon drops, sunflower seeds or mints. Let the habit die of neglect. If you substitute anything for the habit, you will keep it alive and if it is kept alive, you have a good chance of going back to smoking.

Getting exercise is good to do when you quit smoking because it can offset the lowering of the metabolic rate.

When you quit smoking, your body is changing at the cellular and muscular level—your muscles might be sore, but these are temporary and will go away. You probably don't have to do a battery of tests. Almost every symptom you feel will be temporary and should go away.

Nicotine Stresses Out the Heart

If you have quit cold turkey or you are using some form of nicotine replacement, know that nicotine is a vasoconstrictor. When you cut back on nicotine you will get more oxygen into your brain and you might become light headed or dizzy at first because you are not used to having so much oxygen in your brain.

Each time you lower the amount of nicotine in your body you might get dizzy. Be careful driving a car, get up slower than you usually do and just treat yourself like you have just come out of surgery. This is temporary and should go away. You can also do some deep breathing.

11
The Hidden Costs of Quitting Smoking

MANY SMOKERS EXPERIENCE PREDICTABLE, TEMPORARY symptoms when they quit smoking. But you can treat those symptoms inexpensively, without trips to the emergency room or taking a battery of invasive tests.

At the beginning of this book there were quotes from Robin J. and Jenn L. who had quit cold turkey and they had documented all the experiences that they went through to try to get answers and relief by going to the emergency room, consulting with doctors and submitting to all kinds of medical tests. Both Robin and Jenn were prescribed many types of drugs to treat the symptoms of their side effects from quitting smoking.

Let's compare the costs and effectiveness of going to the doctor or emergency room and taking medical tests to using over-the-counter remedies:

Case Study #1
Robin J.—3 trips to the Emergency Room

Symptoms
- Pressure in her chest lower rib cage
- Tightness in the chest and throat
- Trouble breathing
- Sinus and ears hurt
- Anxiety
- Gas
- Heartburn
- Acid reflux
- Sore joints and muscles
- Restless sleep
- Increased need to urinate
- Dizziness
- Blurred vision, floaters
- Hot flashes
- Dry throat
- Tingling in the hands and feet

Tests Given
- Blood panel, EKGs, CAT scan, ultrasound of liver & gallbladder, x-rays of heart, lungs and abdomen, stool sample, vision tests. Test results were all normal.

Diagnosis
- Told she was breathing fine and was just having an anxiety attack.
- Sore throat was diagnosed as Pharyngitis.
- Anxiety
- Ears and Sinus were normal
- Might be in menopause
- Doctors acted like she was going crazy

Treatment Received
- Steroid shots
- Five rounds of antibiotics before doctors decided it was viral.
- Xanax for anxiety
- Prilosec for gas, heartburn and acid reflux
- Zyrtec for sore throat, Pharyngitis

Cost
- 3 trips to emergency room plus prescriptions – $20,420.00

Case Study #2
Jenn L.—Several Doctor Visits

Symptoms
- Constipation
- Bloating
- Fluid retention
- Intestine pain
- Pain in throat
- Pain in hips
- Pain in legs
- Pain in chest
- Pain in back
- High anxiety
- Felt hormonal

Tests Given
- Pelvic ultrasound, several x-rays of chest, thighs and torso. Two complete blood counts plus additional blood work panels.

Diagnosis
- Tests results were all normal
- Some arthritis in her back
- Slightly elevated cholesterol
- She felt like the doctors thought she was crazy

11: THE HIDDEN COSTS OF QUITTING SMOKING

Treatment Received
- No treatment given

Cost
- For several doctors visits $750.00

Case Study #3
Lucy C.—No Doctor Visits

Symptoms
- Sore mouth and gums
- Heartburn
- Gas
- Restless sleep
- Hot flashes
- Irritable
- Anxiety
- Fatigue

Tests Given
- No tests given

Diagnosis
- Understood the symptoms were temporary and would go away

Treatment Received
- Bought the *Kick Butt Recovery Kit* which had all the over the counter remedies that solved the problems.
- For sore mouth, bleeding gums – Life Brand Oral Wound Cleanser
- For heartburn - she took Tums (an anti acid tablet)
- For gas or flatulence - she tried Beano before meals

11: THE HIDDEN COSTS OF QUITTING SMOKING

- For restless sleep - she used Calms Forte
- For hot flashes, irritability and anxiety - she used Pro-Gest
- For fatigue - she took lozenges called Enerjets

Cost

- Total cost for all the over-the-counter remedies $57.00

QUIT SMOKING... GOT SIDE EFFECTS?

Here's a comparison of the costs, tests and results of the three people who quit smoking and how they dealt with the side effects.

	SYMPTOM	TESTS	DIAGNOSIS TREATMENT	COST
ER 3 Trips	Pressure in chest Trouble breathing Sinus & joint pain Anxiety Gas Heartburn Restless sleep Increased urination Dizziness Blurred vision Hot flashes Dry throat Tingling hands/feet	Blood panel EKGs CAT scan Ultrasounds X-rays Stool sample Vision tests	Test results all normal Anxiety attack Pharyngitis Menopause Steroid shots 5 rounds antibiotics Xanax Prilosec Zyrtec	$20,420

11: THE HIDDEN COSTS OF QUITTING SMOKING

	SYMPTOM	TESTS	DIAGNOSIS TREATMENT	COST
Doctor Several visits	Constipation Bloating Anxiety Hormonal Pain in - Intestine Chest Back Legs	Ultrasound X-rays 2 Blood panels	Test results all normal Some arthritis Slightly elevated cholesterol No treatment given	$750
Bought *The Kick Butt Recovery Kit*	Gas Anxiety Fatigue Sore mouth Heartburn Restless sleep Irritable Hot flashes	No tests given Understood symptoms were temporary and would go away	Oral Wound Cleanser Tums Beano Calms Forte Pro-Gest Enerjets	$57

"The information in your book reduced my fears of what I was experiencing. I am a 4th year medical student and I have been smoking heavily since I started university. 4 Days ago I decided to quit and some changes have happened in my body—insomnia, throbbing pain in my legs, toes, hands and even

in the trunk of my body. The pain is episodic and has made me fear that I am sick with cancer or some other disease. I then found your information online and now I understand what's happening. Currently I have neck pains from the spine, could it be due to quitting smoking?"
—Kipkorir Nickson

I wasn't surprised when I read this from a fourth year medical student who was googling how to deal with symptoms of quitting smoking. I asked him if he had any training in his medical school about helping people with smoking cessation and he said no. He had no idea how to help himself with the side effects of quitting smoking that he was suffering from, much less how to help anyone else when he becomes a doctor.

12
Over-the-Counter Remedies for the Side Effects of Quitting Smoking

As you may have noticed with the case studies in the last chapter, the least expensive and most effective treatment for the side effects of quitting smoking is to get over-the-counter remedies like Lucy C. used.

Over the years of teaching smoking cessation I have discovered six main products that are very effective in dealing with the temporary side effects of quitting. There are several problems with recommending these products. One product is made in Canada, another is hard to find, a couple you can order online and a couple you can get in a health food store. You need these products NOW!

The second problem is if you order some of these products now you might have to wait three weeks for them to arrive and the third problem is you might not need the whole box of **Oral Wound Cleanser** or **Pro-Gest**.

So for the first time ever I have bought all the products that I think you will need and split apart the boxes of the products that are individually packaged. I put them together in a kit that you can order from www.Amazon.com or www.ebay.com and start to use the products quickly. Then if you need more of a certain item, then you can order it and start getting relief immediately!

Introducing for the First Time Ever...

Contents of the Kit

- 1 bottle Calms Forte
- 1 bottle Beano
- 1 packet Tums
- 6 packets Pro-Gest
- 8 packets Oral Wound Cleanser
- 6 packets Wake up

12: OVER-THE-COUNTER REMEDIES FOR THE SIDE EFFECTS OF QUITTING SMOKING

Remedy for Gas or Flatulence

Many people get gas or flatulence when they quit smoking. It can be embarrassing. If you take Beano right before your first bite to help stop gas, bloating and discomfort from beans, broccoli, cabbage, onions, peppers, seeds, soy products, whole grains, cereals and carrots. There are many more foods that **may** cause gas so for a complete list of foods that cause gas go to www.beanogas.com/anti-gas-pills.

>Directions for use:
>Swallow 2 or 3 tablets right before your first bite of problem food.
>
>Ingredients:
>Alpha galactosidase enzyme 300 galU (derived from Aspergillus niger)
>
>Other ingredients:
>Cellulose gel, Mannitol, Invertase, Potato Starch, Magnesium Stearate, Colloidal Silica, Gelatin.
>
>Contains: Cod, Flounder, Redfish
>
>See more at:
>www.beanogas.com/anti-gas-pills
>
>The kit includes a bottle of Beano To Go containing 12 tablets.

Remedy for Heartburn or Acid Indigestion

Tums is common in the United States but it needs to be part of this recovery kit because acid indigestion is so common.

It relieves acid indigestion, heartburn, sour stomach and upset stomach.

Ingredients: Calcium Carbonate

Remedy for Anxiety, Water Retention

Pro-Gest made by Emerita and is a natural progesterone balancing cream.

Ingredients:
Purified water, tocopheryl Acetate (vitamin E), Aloe Barbadensis (Aloe Vera) Leaf Juice, Carthamus Tinctorius (Hybrid Safflower) seed oil, Panthemol, Glycerin, Prunus Amygdalus Dulcis (Sweet Almond) oil, Glyceryl Stearate, Cetyl Alcohol, Sodium Behemoyl Lactylate, Stearic Acid, USP Progesterone, Pnenoxyethanol, Caprylyl Glycol, Sorbic Acid, Carbomer, Potassium Hydroxide.

Directions:
Rub in 1 pea size amount of the cream into the fatty parts of your body twice a day. One packet may last more than one day.

12: OVER-THE-COUNTER REMEDIES FOR THE SIDE EFFECTS OF QUITTING SMOKING

A Homeopathic Remedy for Insomnia

Calms Forte is made by Hylands. When people quit smoking sleep may be affected temporarily. I learned about Calm Forte from a naturopathic doctor. It is made from homeopathic products and is over-the-counter and not habit forming.

I have tried prescribed sleeping pills and they always made me feel groggy and then I tried other sleeping remedies like Melatonin and that didn't work. I don't need a sleep aid very often but I have recommended these to my students and even my mother!

Ingredients:
Passiflora 1x | Triple Strength HPUS: For restless sleep from exhaustion. Avena Sativa 1x | Double Strength HPUS: For stress, nervousness. Humulus Lupulus 1x | Double Strength HPUS: For sleeplessness. Chamomilla 2x | HPUS: For nervous irritability.

And the following biochemic phosphates for enhancing cellular function: Calcarea Phosphorica 3x HPUS, Ferrum Phosphoricum 3x HPUS, Kali Phosphoricum 3x HPUS, Natrum Phosphoricum 3x HPUS, Magnesia PhosphoMarianericum 3x HPUS

Directions:
Swallow one or two pills as needed.
The kit will include a 32 pill bottle.

Help for Fatigue

Nicotine is a stimulant. It makes your heart beat up to 10,000 times more per day. When you stop using nicotine, you don't get that punch of nicotine and it makes some people really tired.

Your body is switching from an artificial punch of nicotine to natural and in the process it can almost be dangerous if you are going to drive a car or work heavy machinery.

Enerjets is like drinking a cup of coffee. It works up to 3 times faster than energy drinks.

Ingredients:
Sugar, corn syrup, glycerine caffeine, powdered instant coffee, acesulfame-K, propylene glycol, powdered licorice extract, natural and artificial flavors, FD& C Yellow #6, FD & C Blue #2, FD &C Red #40

Calories: 15

A normal bag comes with 12 caffeinated drops but I am sending 6 in the kit. They are individually wrapped.

12: OVER-THE-COUNTER REMEDIES FOR THE SIDE EFFECTS OF QUITTING SMOKING

Remedy for Sore Mouth and Gums

Some smokers experience sore, burning or inflamed mouth and gums. Here is a mouthwash to treat: gingivitis, canker sores, denture irritation, orthodontic irritation, minor oral injuries and soreness after minor dental procedures.

The original box of Life brand Oral Wound Cleanser comes in with 20 individual packets. I am including 8 in the kit. You can always order more from the company.

Ingredients:
Sodium Perborate Monohydrate. Tartaric acid (sodium Bitartrate), sodium saccharin, Natural peppermint flavor, Natural vanilla flavor

Directions:
Dissolve one packet in warm water and gargle. Do not swallow. Swish solutions around mouth for at least 1 minute.

For best results do not take food or water for 20 minutes after rinsing. This gives you a refreshing, soothing, healing feeling in your mouth.

To order the Kick Butt Recovery Kit go to Amazon and look for Kick Butt Recovery Kit or go to www.kickbuttrecovery.com and look for the link for the kit.

Remedy for Getting Rid of Wrinkles

I have tested all the products that I recommend with thousands of students since 1978. There is one group of products that I will need Beta testers for and that is how to get rid of wrinkles from years of smoking.

Email if you are interested in being in a test group to eliminate wrinkles whether you are a smoker or non-smoker at easeout@nicotinesolutions.com

13
Resources

This Bonus will make this book come alive!!
I was going to charge for this membership site but I decided it is going to be free of charge! Go to www.KickButtRecovery.com

Here's what you get:
- All the Side Effects explained on videos
- Weekly webinars – ask any questions that you are wondering about
- Guest speakers on various topics like anxiety, insomnia, heartburn, etc.

If you are still smoking

KEEP SMOKING WHILE YOU LEARN TO QUIT!

'The Quit Queen'

NO *Drugs!*
NO *Side Effects!*
NO *Weight Gain!*

You Are Invited to a Free Live Training
at www.TheQuitQueen.com

Helping thousands of smokers
quit smoking internationally for over 25 years

Facebook Groups

There are 6 Facebook Groups that have been set up to support you for free in quitting smoking.

It is best for you to join the main group "Dealing With the Side Effects of Quitting Smoking" and then if you fit into another group that would be a smaller group for specific support that is more targeted to your needs.

The groups are listed in the following pages:

13: RESOURCES

Dealing With The Side Effects Of Quitting Smoking

You have quit smoking and you are struggling with some side effects from quitting smoking. You could use some support to deal with the side effects.

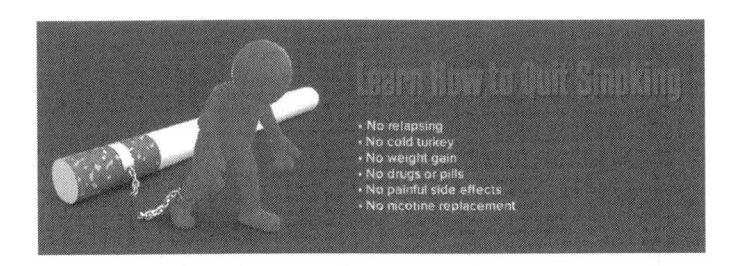

Learn How To Quit Smoking Without Drugs Or Side Effects

With a little bit a preparation you can quit smoking with:
- No relapsing
- No cold turkey
- No weight gain
- No drugs or pills
- No painful side effects
- No nicotine replacement

How To Quit Smoking When You Are Pregnant

If you are pregnant or planning to get pregnant you do need to quit smoking.

The doctor will tell you to quit right away, but it is better to give the body and mind a little bit of planning.

Going cold turkey can be very shocking to your system. You certainly don't want to use any drugs like Chantix or Wellbutrin or any kind of nicotine replacement therapy like the gum, patch or lozenges.

Join this Facebook Group and you can get guidance on how to quit smoking permanently without drugs, side effects or weight gain.

13: RESOURCES

How To Quit Smoking During Menopause Without Side Effects And Get Help With The Symptoms of Menopause

You CAN quit smoking calmly and comfortably during menopause if you know how. It is best not to use any drugs or pills to quit smoking during menopause.

With a little bit of preparation you can quit calmly and comfortably and find solutions to your issues with menopause as well.

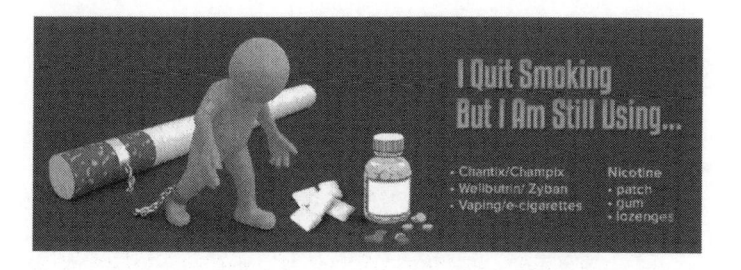

I Have Quit Smoking But I Am Still Using

Chantix/Champix
Wellbutrin/Zyban
Vaping/E-cigarettes

Nicotine
Patches
Gum
Lozenges

If you are using any of these products you are still hooked on nicotine or the smoking habit in some way. You have quit smoking but you still need help with the side effects and withdrawal from the drugs or the nicotine replacement.

I Have Quit Smoking! Dealing With The Side Effects Of Quitting Smoking During Menopause

I have quit smoking and I realize that menopause symptoms mimic the symptoms of quitting smoking.

I need help to sort out which symptoms are from menopause and which are from quitting smoking such as night sweats, insomnia, heartburn, anxiety etc!!!

QUIT SMOKING... GOT SIDE EFFECTS?

7 Tips to Quit Smoking

OLD	VS	NEW
1. Change Mindset		
Willpower		Train Subconscious
2. Detoxify		
Cold Turkey		Smoke While Quitting
3. Don't Feed the Habit		
Substitute Food		Don't Substitute
4. Learn to Cope		
Stressed		Handle Stress
5. Change Behaviors		
Think About Cigarettes		Change Habits
6. Recovery Symptoms		
Doctor Trips		No Doctor Trips
7. Support Group		
By Yourself		Group Support

Lela Bryan   www.nicotinesolutions.com   easeout@nicotinesolutions.com   425-444-6616

13: RESOURCES

7 Tips to Quit

1. Instead of using will power—which is cold turkey—you need to change your mindset and train your subconscious to quit.
2. Allow yourself time instead of an abrupt cessation—you need to detoxify slowly and smoke while you quit.
3. Apply weight controls instead of substituting food for the habit.
4. Address the stress—instead of being stressed about quitting ease your stress through a variety of techniques.
5. Need to change your behaviors instead of always thinking about cigarettes you need to change your thinking and handle stress in a different way.
6. Change your habits.
7. Instead of trips to the doctors—find a support group and do not try to do this on your own.

To actually put these tips into practice and start to change your habits you are invited to attend a Free Live Training. Just go to:
www.TheQuitQueen.com

Lela Bryan, also known as "The Quit Queen"

About the Author

Lela Bryan, founder and Chief Learning Officer of Nicotine Solutions, quit smoking—happily and permanently—on June 4, 1978. She has been successfully teaching others how to quit smoking and chewing ever since!

Originally a high school teacher, Lela found her true calling when—after 16 years of smoking—she finally discovered a way to quit that actually worked.

Determined to spread the word, Lela decided to leave the school system and use her teaching skills to help people quit smoking instead. Since then, she has taught smoking cessation throughout the US, Canada, France, England, Bulgaria, Australia, New Zealand and South Africa. And she has continued to hone and refine her program over the years to make it as effective and cutting edge as possible.

Originally all of Lela's classes took place in person. But with the advent of the Internet she saw a way to help even more people stop smoking, regain their health and realize their dreams. Today she uses a combination of telephone conferencing, email, video, and audio technologies to deliver impressive results.

Thanks to her innovative approaches, Lela's students consistently experience the highest success rates of any system in the world—90% of her students stop smoking by the end of the program.

With the Nicotine Solutions program, Lela can help anyone; anywhere quit smoking or chewing (or any other nicotine addiction) easily and permanently.

All you need is a telephone and an internet connection and you can learn to stop smoking or chewing anywhere in the world without side effects, gaining weight or using drugs.

Lela Bryan Contact Information

easeout@nicotinesolutions.com
425-444-6616 USA Alameda, CA (Pacific Time)
Skype: easeout

Also, if you have other ideas on how to cope with the side effects or want to email me or call me with comments, I would love to hear from you!

Although I have been teaching people how to quit smoking since 1978 my recommendations are not intended to replace sound medical advice.

Made in the USA
Lexington, KY
29 March 2019